junie b. jones®

Is Not a Crook

KB259729

by BARBARA PARK

illustrated by

Denise Brunkus

Long tail Books

Junie B. Jones Is Not a Crook

ISBN 979-11-91343-16-8 14740

Longtail, Inc.

Contents

1
No Good Reason

My name is Junie B. Jones. The B **stand**s **for** Beatrice. **Except** I don't like Beatrice. I just like B and **that's all**.

Here is a story for you.

It is called "Once Upon a Time My Grandfather Named Frank Miller Went to the Store and He Bought Me Some **Mitten**s."

Once upon a time my grandfather named

Frank Miller went to the store and he bought me some mittens. They are made out of black ***furry fur.***

And guess what? It was not even my birthday! Or Christmas! Or Valentine's Day![1] *Plus the mittens were not even on sale!*

Grampa Miller just bought them for no good reason! And that is the bestest[2] *reason I ever heard of!*

That's how come I love that guy very much.

Plus also he can ***skip.***

The end.

---

1 **Valentine's Day** 밸런타인데이. 성 발렌티누스 사제의 순교를 기리는 2월 14일을 이르는 말. 해마다 이날이 되면 사랑하는 사람끼리 선물이나 카드를 주고받는 풍습이 있다.

2 **bestest** 단어 'best(최고의)'를 강조한 비격식적인 표현. '최고로 좋은'이라는 뜻을 나타내며 어린아이가 주로 사용한다.

I like that story a real lot.

'Cause guess why?

I didn't even **make** it **up**, that's why!

That **adventure** actually happened to me! My grampa[3] Miller really *did* buy me mittens for no good reason!

And they are **gorgeous**, I tell you!

When I first opened them, I got filled with **glee**.

Glee is when you run. And jump. And skip. And laugh. And **clap**. And dance on top of the dining room table.

Then your mother takes you down from the table. And she carries you to your room for a ***time-out***.

---

3 **grampa** '할아버지(grandpa)'를 부르는 말로, 'gramp', 'grampa', 'grampy' 등 다양한 표현이 있다.

Time-outs kill the glee.

I wore my new mittens the whole **entire** morning. Plus also I wore them to afternoon **kindergarten**.

I wore them with my **attractive** winter jacket. Only it wasn't actually cold out. Only who even cares? 'Cause that **outfit** looked very beautiful together.

I showed my mittens to my bestest friend named Grace. Also, I showed them to a **variety** of strangers.

After I got to school, I held my hands over my head. And I runned[4] all over the **playground**.

---

4 **runned** (ran) 영어권 국가의 아이들이 동사의 과거형을 말할 때 모든 단어의 끝에 '-ed'를 붙이는 실수를 종종 한다. 이 책에 나오는 'thinked(thought)', 'lighted(lit)' 등이 이와 같은 경우이다.

"LOOK, EVERYBODY! LOOK AT MY NEW MITTENS! MY GRAMPA FRANK MILLER BOUGHT THEM FOR NO GOOD REASON!"

I **wave**d them all around in the air.

"HOW MANY CHILDREN SEE THESE LOVELY THINGS? RAISE YOUR HANDS," I **holler**ed.

Nobody raised their hands.

"HOW MANY CHILDREN THINK THESE MITTENS ARE GORGEOUS? PLEASE COME FORWARD!" I **yell**ed.

Nobody came forward.

I put my hands back down and walked to that Grace.

"I couldn't **create** any interest," I said very **glum**.

Only guess what? Just then, I **spot**ted my other bestest friend named Lucille!

I ran my fastest to **greet** her.

"LUCILLE! LUCILLE! LOOK AT MY GORGEOUS NEW MITTENS! SEE THEM? THEY ARE MADE OUT OF BLACK

FURRY FUR!"

Lucille **pet**ted them.

"My family has *lots* of fur," she said. "My mother has a fur **cape**. And my aunt has a fur jacket. And my uncle has a fur hat. Plus my **nanna** just bought a **brand-new** mink coat.[5] Only she can't wear it outside the house. Or else people will throw paint on her."

My mouth came **all the way** open.

"Why, Lucille? Why will people throw paint on your nanna?" I asked.

Lucille **cross**ed **her arms**.

"Don't you know *anything*, Junie B. Jones? It's because people who love furry

---

5 **mink coat** 족제빗과의 동물인 밍크의 털로 만든 코트.

animals don't like them being made into coats for nannas."

Just then, I felt **relief** in me. 'Cause I'm not even a nanna, that's why. And besides, my mittens aren't even made out of *real* furry animals. They are made out of ***fake*** furry animals. And those kind don't even **count**.

All of a sudden, the bell rang for school.

I **zoom**ed to my room like a **speed**ing rocket.

'Cause guess why?

More people to show my mittens to!

That's why!

2
Fur Hands

I showed my **mitten**s to my teacher.

Her name is Mrs.

She has another name, too. But I just like Mrs. and **that's all**.

"Feel them, Mrs.," I said. "Feel how soft they are."

I **rub**bed them on her face.

"Oooh, they *are* soft, Junie B.," she said. "Be sure and put them in your jacket pockets so they won't get lost, okay?"

I **skip**ped very happy to my seat.

"Yeah, only I'm not even going to lose them," I said to just myself. "I am going to wear them right on my hands. The whole **livelong** day. 'Cause I love these guys, that's why."

I took off my **attractive** winter jacket. And sat down at my table.

Then I **tap**ped on Lucille with my **furry** mittens.

"Hello. How are you today? I have fur hands. See them, Lucille? See my hands of fur?"

I flew them in the air.

"This is what fur hands look like when they're flying in the air," I said.

I **wave**d hello.

"This is what fur hands look like when they're waving hello," I said.

Lucille did a **frown**.

"You're being **annoy**ing," she said.

That's how come I turned around. And I smiled at a boy named William.

"I have fur hands, William. See them? See my fur hands?"

I tapped on his head.

"This is what fur hands look like when they're tapping you on your head," I said.

Just then, I got up from my chair. And I skipped to my boyfriend named Ricardo.

I **tickle**d him under the **chin** with my

softy[1] hands of fur.

"This is what fur hands look like when

1 **softy** 단어 'soft(부드러운)'를 주니 B.가 'softy'라고 장난스럽게 말한 표현.

they're tickling you under your chin," I said.

Then I **grin**ned and grinned. 'Cause that boy **bring**s **out** the best in me. That's why.

Pretty soon, Mrs. saw me out of my seat.

She held my hand and **march**ed me back to my table.

"This is how fur hands look when they're marching to my table," I said.

Mrs. **plop**ped me in my chair.

Then she pulled off my fur hands. And she put them on her desk.

I did a sad **sigh**.

"That is how fur hands look when they're no longer in my **possess**ion," I **whisper**ed to just myself.

After that, I put my head on my desk.

And **cover**ed up with my arms.

And I didn't come out for a real long time.

3
Being Brownie

Mrs. said I could have my mittens back at **recess**.

I **stare**d and stared at the clock. Then I **tap**ped my fingers on my table. And I did loud breaths.

Lucille **tattletaled**[1] on me.

"Junie B. keeps tapping her fingers and

1 **tattletale** 주로 명사 또는 형용사로 쓰이는 단어 'tattletale(고자질쟁이, 고자질하는)'을 여기에서는 '고자질하다'라는 의미의 동사처럼 사용했다.

making loud breaths! And I can't even **concentrate** on my work!" she **grouch**ed.

Mrs. came to my table.

"Hello. How are you today?" I said kind of nervous. "I am fine. **Except** I don't actually have my mittens."

She tapped her foot real fast.

That was not a good **sign**, I think.

Only guess what? Just then, the bell rang for recess!

"OH BOY![2]" I **yell**ed. "OH BOY! OH BOY! 'CAUSE NOW I CAN HAVE MY MITTENS BACK! RIGHT, MRS.? RIGHT? RIGHT?"

I **zoom**ed to her desk and put them on

---

2 **boy** 여기에서는 '소년'이라는 뜻이 아니라, '맙소사' 또는 '어머나'라는 의미로 놀람이나 기쁨 등을 나타내는 표현으로 쓰였다.

my hands.

Then I **rub**bed those softy things all over my **cheek**s.

"It's good to be with you again," I **whisper**ed into their fur.

After that, I put on my attractive winter jacket. And I skipped outside with my friends.

Me and tattletale Lucille and that Grace play horses together at recess.

I am Brownie. Lucille is Blackie. And that Grace is Yellowie.

"I'M YELLOWIE!" shouted that Grace.

"I'M BLACKIE!" shouted Lucille.

"I'M BROWNIE!" I shouted.

Only just then, I looked at my mittens.

I did a **frown**.

'Cause there was a little bit of a problem here, I think.

"Yeah, only how can I even be Brownie? 'Cause my horse **paw**s are black. And so I am two different colors, **apparent**ly."

Lucille and that Grace did frowns, too.

"Hmm," said that Grace.

"Hmm," said Lucille.

"Hmm," I said.

Just then, that Grace **clap**ped her hands together very excited. "*I* know, Junie B.! Today you and Lucille can ***trade!*** Today *Lucille* can be Brownie! And *you* can be Blackie! And so that way your horse paws will be the right color!"

Me and Lucille looked and looked at that girl. 'Cause what kind of crazy idea was that?

I did a **huffy** breath.

"Yeah, only how can I even be *Blackie* when I am already *Brownie,* Grace?" I said. "I have been Brownie for my whole **entire career**. You can't just go *changing,* you know."

"Yeah, Grace. You can't just go *changing,*" said Lucille.

That Grace looked **embarrass**ed at herself. "Oh yeah . . . What was I thinking?" she said very **mumbling**.

After that, all of us sat down in the grass. And we tapped on our **chin**s.

We thinked and thinked and thinked.

Then—**all of a sudden**—my whole face **light**ed up.

"Hey! I thought of it! I thought of it! I

know **'zact**ly what to do!" I shouted.

I jumped up.

"Start again, Grace! Say your name again! Say that you are Yellowie!"

That Grace looked **curious** at me.

"I'm Yellowie," she said.

I pointed to Lucille.

"I'm Blackie," she said next.

I **spin**ned around real **joyful**.

"I'M BROWNIE!" I shouted. "ONLY GUESS WHAT? YESTERDAY MY GRAMPA BROWNIE BOUGHT ME BLACK FURRY MITTENS! AND SO THAT IS HOW COME I AM TWO DIFFERENT COLORS, APPARENTLY!"

After that, all of us did **high five**s. And we started playing horses.

We **gallop**ed. And **trot**ted. And **snort**ed. And **snuffle**d.

Only too bad for me. 'Cause the sun kept on **beat**ing **down** on my horse head. And I got **drip**pity[3] inside my attractive winter jacket.

"I am going to die from heat **perspiration**," I said.

That's how come I trotted over to a tree.

---

3 **drippity** 주니 B.가 만들어 낸 말로, 단어 'drip(방울방울 흐르다, 뚝뚝 떨어지다)'을 활용하여 '방울방울 흐르는, 뚝뚝 떨어지는'이라는 의미의 형용사로 사용하였다.

And I took off all my **stuff**.

First I took off my attractive winter jacket. Then I took off my furry black mittens. And I **pile**d them in a **careful** pile.

After that, I galloped away to find my horse friends. And we played and played.

Pretty soon, Mrs. **blew** her loud **whistle**.

That means the end of recess.

"COMING!" shouted Yellowie.

"COMING!" shouted Blackie.

"COMING!" I shouted.

Then I hurried up back to the tree to get my stuff.

Only guess what?

I saw something very terrible there, that's what!

And it's called *HEY!!! SOMEBODY* ***STOLE****D MY MITTENS!!!!!*

4
No Teddy Backpack

I runned all around the tree.

"911! 911! 911!" I **holler**d. "SOMEBODY **STOLE**D THEM! SOMEBODY STOLED MY **MITTENS**!"

Mrs. came very quick.

"THEY STOLED THEM! THEY STOLED MY MITTENS! 911!" I shouted some more.

Mrs. **bend**ed down next to me. *"Who,* Junie B.? Who stole them?" she asked.

"A stealer, that's who! A stealer stoled them! And so what kind of school is this? 'Cause I didn't even know there was **crook**s at this place!"

Mrs. said **calm** down my voice.

"Yeah, only I can't even calm it down that good. 'Cause I am **heartsick**, that's why."

Heartsick is the **grown-up** word for when your heart is sick.

I looked at the ground real sad. "Now all I have left is my **dumb attractive** jacket."

Mrs. picked it up. Then she holded my hand. And me and her started to walk.

"You and I are going to the office," she told me.

I quick tried to get my hand away from

her.

"No, Mrs.! I'm not allowed to go there! Mother said if I get sended to the office one more time, I will get ***groun**ded, young lady."*

Tears came in my eyes.

"Grounded, young lady, is when I have to stay on my own ground," I said. "Plus also I can go on the **rug**."

Mrs. smiled. "I'm not taking you to the **principal**'s office to ***punish*** you, Junie B.," she said. "I'm taking you to find your mittens."

I did a **gasp**.

"Principal?" I asked very shocked. "Principal stoled my mittens?"

Mrs. laughed real loud.

"No, Junie B. He didn't steal your mittens. The office is where the Lost and Found[1] is **locate**d."

After that, she took my hand again. And we hurried up to the office.

There is a **grouchy typing** lady at that place.

I am not **fond** of her.

"Junie B. needs to look through the Lost and Found," Mrs. told her. "Please send her back to class when she's finished."

Then Mrs. went back to Room Nine and left me there all **by myself**.

The typing lady looked over the **counter** at me.

---

1 **Lost and Found** 분실물 보관소. 사람들이 잃어버린 물건을 관리하기 위해 모아 두는 장소.

I did a **gulp**.

"Yeah, only I'm not even bad today," I explained very nervous. "Somebody stoled my mittens. And that is the end of my **tale**."

The typing lady kept on looking at me. She didn't say any words.

Sweat came on my head.

"Whew . . . it's **warmish** in here, isn't it?" I said.

Just then, I heard a door open.

It was Principal!

He was coming out of his office!

I jumped up and down at his **sight**. 'Cause I know that guy very good!

"Principal! Look! Look! It's me! It's Junie B. Jones! My mittens got stoled on the **playground**! And so Mrs. brought me here to get them! So just hand them over and I will be **on my way** . . . no questions asked."

Principal looked funny at me. Then he went to the **closet** and pulled out a big box.

"This is the Lost and Found, Junie B.," he explained. "Anytime that someone finds something that's been lost, they bring it here. And we put it in this box."

"How come?" I asked. "How come they bring it here **instead** of taking it home? 'Cause one time I found a nickel[2] in the street. And Daddy said I could put it in my

---

2 **nickel** 니켈. 미국이나 캐나다에서 쓰이는 5센트(cent)짜리 동전.

bank. 'Cause *finding* isn't the same thing as *stealing*. Right, Principal? Finding is a *lucky duck*.[3]"

Principal laughed a little bit.

"Well, finding a nickel in the street is different, Junie B.," he said. "For one thing, it would be almost **impossible** to **discover** who the owner of the nickel really was. And for another thing, losing a nickel isn't really a **big deal**. But when someone loses something ***personal***—like mittens, for instance—well, that's a *very* big deal. And so if someone else *finds* the mittens, they can bring them to the Lost and Found, and the owner can get them back."

---

3 **lucky duck** 굉장히 운이 좋은 사람을 이르는 말.

He smiled.

"And that makes everyone happy, Junie B.," he said. "The owner is happy because she has her mittens back. And the person who found them is happy because she's done a good **deed**."

He pointed to a piece of paper taped on the box.

"See this? This is a **poem** the third **grade** wrote about the Lost and Found. It says:

*"If you find **stuff**,*
Bring it in.
All day long,
*You'll wear a **grin**."*

I did a frown.

"Yeah, only here's the problem. I didn't *lose* my mittens. They got stoled **on *purpose***. And so no one will bring them in and wear a grin, probably."

Principal raised up his **eyebrow**s. "Well, you never know, Junie B. Why don't you look in there and see?"

He opened up the box for me.

That's when my eyes got big and wide.

'Cause it was filled with the wonderfulest[4] items I ever saw!

There were sweaters! And sweatshirts![5] And baseball caps! And gloves! And

---

4 **wonderfulest** 형용사 'wonderful'의 최상급을 잘못 만든 것으로, 올바른 표현은 'most wonderful'이다.

5 **sweatshirt** 스웨트 셔츠. 신축성 있고 땀을 잘 흡수하는 소재로 만든 운동복 상의.

balls! And a lunchbox! And a scarf! And sunglasses! And a watch with Mickey Mouse[6] on it!

Also, there was a backpack that looked like a teddy bear![7]

"OOOOH! I ALWAYS WANTED ONE OF THESE!" I hollered real **thrill**ed.

I put it on my back and **skip**ped around the office.

"How does it look back there?" I asked.

Principal runned after me.

He took the teddy off my back. And put it back in the box.

---

6 **Mickey Mouse** 미키 마우스. 미국의 유명 영화 제작사 디즈니(Disney)가 만든 가장 대표적인 만화 주인공. 검고 둥근 귀를 지닌 쥐로 노란 단추가 달린 빨간 바지를 입은 것이 특징이다.

7 **teddy bear** 테디 베어. 장난감 곰 인형으로, 미국의 26대 대통령 테어도어 루스벨트(Theodore Roosevelt)의 애칭을 따서 만들었다.

If you find stuff,
Bring it in.
All day long,
You'll wear a grin.

"We're looking for your *mittens,* remember?"

Just then, I felt **upset** again. 'Cause I almost forgot about those **furry** guys, that's why.

"Oh, yeah . . . my mittens," I said real **glum**.

I looked through the box some more.

"They're not here," I said. "My mittens are gone forever and ever, I think."

I did a sad **sigh**.

Then I picked up the teddy backpack again.

"Maybe I will take *this* instead," I said. "'Cause this teddy backpack will **ease** my pain, I believe."

Principal said no.

"How come?" I asked. "'Cause the owner doesn't even want it anymore, I **bet**. Her mother already bought her a new teddy backpack, probably. And so this one is just going to go to **waste**."

Principal stood me up and turned me to the door.

That meant I am leaving, I think.

"Come back tomorrow and look for your mittens again," he said.

I talked real fast.

"Yeah, only I just remembered something. I used to have a teddy backpack just like that one, maybe. Only then I lost it, probably. And so I better take that one home with me. Or else my mother might be mad."

Principal walked me to the door. He faced me down the **hall**.

"Good-bye, Junie B.," he said.

I hanged my head real **disappoint**ed.

'Cause guess why?

Good-bye means *no teddy backpack.*

5
Gargling and Scribbling

Room Nine is way far from **Principal**'s office.

I had to stop at the **water fountain**. Or else I might not **make it**.

I **press**ed the water button with my **thumb**.

Then I **pucker**ed up my **lip**s. And I **suck**ed the water in.

I didn't even put my mouth on the

spout. 'Cause there's lip **dirt** on that thing of course.

I **slosh**ed the water all around in my **cheek**s.

Then I **bend**ed my head way back. And I did some gargles.

I can gargle very perfect. **Except** I can't keep the water in my actual mouth.

It runned out the sides and **dribble**d on the floor.

I **splash**ed in it with my toe.

That's when I saw something very wonderful down there.

"Hey! It's one of those pens that writes four different colors!" I said.

I quick picked it up and pushed the little red button on the top.

A red pen **pop**ped out the bottom.

I scribbled red scribble all over my hand.

"Wowie wow wow! I *love* this thing!" I

said.

After that, I pushed the green button and scribbled green scribble. And I pushed the blue button and scribbled blue scribble. Plus also I pushed the black button and scribbled black scribble.

"This pen makes scribbling a **pleasure**," I said.

I put it in my pocket and started skipping to Room Nine.

Only too bad for me. 'Cause **all of a sudden**, I remembered about the Lost and Found.

I stopped.

"Oh no. I wish I didn't even remember about that," I said. "Now I have to take my pen to the Lost and Found. Or else I won't wear a grin."

I did a **frown**. 'Cause something didn't **make sense** here, that's why.

"Yeah, only I was already *wearing* a grin," I said. "I weared a grin as soon as I *saw* this wonderful thing. And so taking it to the office will only make me sad."

I **tap**ped on my **chin**.

"Hmm. Maybe Principal is a little **mixed up** about this," I said to just myself. "I'm pretty sure I will be happier if I keep it.

"And here's another thing I am thinking. I am thinking whoever owned this pen didn't even **take** good **care of** it. So I will give it a good home. And so what can be a gooder[1] **deed** than that?"

I took it out of my pocket and looked at

it.

"Plus this even makes sense. 'Cause first I got my mittens stolen. And then I couldn't have the teddy **backpack**. And so keeping this pen is **fair** and **square**."

All of a sudden, my whole face **light**ed up. 'Cause I just thought of a *different* **poem**, that's why!

And it is called *Finders keepers, losers* ***weep**ers!*

"Finders keepers, losers weepers!" I said real **thrill**ed. "Finders keepers, losers weepers!"

Then I jumped up and down very happy. 'Cause everybody says that! And so

---

1 **gooder** 형용사 'good'의 비교급을 잘못 만든 것으로, 올바른 표현은 'better'이다.

Finders keepers is really the **rule**, I **bet**!

After that, I put my pen back in my pocket.

And I skipped the rest of the way to Room Nine.

6
My Grampa's Wallet

I kept my pen in my pocket the whole rest of the day.

I didn't want people to see it. Or else they might **tattletale** to Mrs. And she would make me take it to the Lost and Found.

I behaved myself very good. 'Cause I didn't want to **'tract 'tention**, that's why.

I kept my hand in my pocket so my

pen would not fall out.

Also, I kept thinking about my **mittens**. 'Cause I still missed those **furry** guys.

I put my head down on my table.

"Maybe my grampa Miller might buy me some *more* furry mittens," I **whisper**ed. "'Cause that would be a perfect solution, I think."

I raised up my head.

"Hey, yeah! Then I would have wonderful new mittens, *plus* a wonderful new pen. And so what more can a girl ask for? That's what I'd like to know!"

I sat up in my chair and **tap**ped on Lucille.

"Guess what, Lucille? Maybe my grampa Frank Miller might buy me some new mittens. And then all my troubles will be over."

Lucille said *whoop-de-do*[1] for me.

"I know it is *whoop-de-do,*" I said real thrilled. "And so, thank you for your **support**."

After school, me and my bestest friend named Grace rode the bus together.

I runned home from my corner like a **speedy bullet**.

My grampa Frank Miller was **babysit**ting my brother named Ollie.

"GRAMPA FRANK MILLER! GRAMPA FRANK MILLER! WE GOTTA GO TO

1 **whoop-de-do** 본래 '야단법석', '대소동'이라는 뜻이지만, 여기에서는 운율을 이용한 일종의 감탄사처럼 쓰였다.

THE MITTEN STORE! WE GOTTA GO TO THE MITTEN STORE!" I **holler**ed real loud.

Grampa Frank Miller was in the living room **rock**ing Ollie.

He looked funny at me.

"Go *where?*" he asked.

"TO THE MITTEN STORE! TO THE MITTEN STORE! WE GOTTA GO TO THE MITTEN STORE!"

I pulled on his hand.

"GET UP! GET UP! LET'S GET A **WIGGLE** ON!"

Grampa Miller looked **confuse**d at me.

That's how come I had to sit down. And I told him what happened at school.

"Someone **stoled** my mittens," I said. "They stoled them while I was being Brownie. And I didn't even know there were **crooks** at that place."

Grampa Frank Miller shook his head very sad.

"I guess you can find crooks almost anywhere, honey," he said.

"I know it," I told him. "That's how come I'm never going to see those furry guys again. And so you and me have to go to the mitten store."

I felt in his back pocket. Then I danced around real thrilled.

"**Hurray**!" I shouted. "Hurray for your

big fat wallet! 'Cause you got **cash** in there. Right, Grampa? Right? Right?"

Grampa Frank Miller laughed.

"Yes, I do. I've got cash all right," he said. "But I'm afraid we won't be able to buy you more mittens. The mittens I bought you were the only furry ones they had left. I bought the very last **pair**."

Just then, all the happy went right out of me. 'Cause I didn't actually **count on** this terrible **development**.

"Yeah, only we *have* to, Grampa. We *have* to buy more furry mittens. Or else what will I even do?"

Grampa Miller **ruffle**d my hair.

"Did you look in the Lost and Found at school?" he asked.

I did a sad breath. "Yeah, only that **dumb** thing doesn't work that good. 'Cause people don't always **turn stuff in**."

I **pat**ted my new pen in my pocket.

"Trust me on this," I said real soft.

"Well, your mittens could still **turn up**," he said. "**Folk**s will surprise you sometimes."

Then he told me a story about his wallet.

"A few years ago I lost my wallet at the mall. I was sure I would never ever see it again," he said.

I **bob**bed my head up and down. "I know it. That's because of *Finders keepers, losers* ***weep****ers*," I said. "*Finders keepers, losers weepers* is the **rule**. Right, Grampa?"

Grampa Miller smiled.

"Well, it might be the rule for *some* people," he said. "But luckily, it's not the rule for *everyone*. Because the very next day—when I went out to get my mail—there it was! My wallet was sitting right **smack** in the middle of my **mailbox**! And not one single penny[2] was missing!"

His eyes looked happy and **sparkly**.

"Can you **imagine** that, little girl?" he asked. "Someone had the chance to take everything in my wallet. But **instead**, they drove **all the way** to my house. And they put it in my mailbox."

Just then, he **reach**ed in his back pocket and pulled out his wallet.

"Look what I would have lost if they hadn't returned it," he said.

He took a picture out of his wallet. And handed it to me.

"It's you and a baby," I said.

"But that's not just *any* baby," he said. "That's *you,* Junie B.! That's a picture of the very first time I ever held you."

---

2 **penny** 페니. 미국의 화폐 단위인 센트(1달러의 100분의 1)를 부르는 다른 이름. 아주 적은 잔돈이나 푼돈이라는 의미로도 사용한다.

He took the picture back and **stare**d and stared at it.

"Nicest thing a stranger ever did for me . . . bringing this picture back," he whispered real soft.

Then he **lean**ed over again.

And he kissed me on my head.

7
The Pink Fluffy Girl

After I talked to my grampa, I went to my room.

I closed my door real secret.

Then I took my wonderful pen out of my pocket. And I did a big **sigh**.

'Cause I had **confusion** in me, that's why.

"I wish I never even heard that wallet story," I said. "'Cause *Finders keepers, losers*

weepers isn't the **rule, apparent**ly. And so now maybe I might be a crook."

I looked at my wonderful pen.

"Yeah, only I don't even *feel* like a crook. I feel like a lucky duck. But I still have to take this thing to the Lost and Found, probably. And then it will go to **waste** just like the teddy **backpack**."

All of a sudden, I heard Mother and Daddy come home from work.

I quick hided my pen under my mattress.[1] 'Cause those two would not be understanding of this situation.

They came in my room and kissed me hello.

---

1 **mattress** 매트리스. 속에 스프링이나 스펀지 등을 넣어 푹신하게 만든 침대용 깔개 또는 두툼한 침구.

I told them what happened to my **mitten**s.

Then I **beg**ged and begged for them to take me to the store. But Mother said *there's no more left*. And Daddy said *there's no more left,* too. And so there was no more left, apparently.

That's how come I got **depress**ed all over again. And I couldn't even sleep good that night.

I kept on wondering about who was the mitten crook. And what did he look like. 'Cause I've seen crooks on TV before. And they are **biggish** and **mean**ish[2] with

2 **meanish** 주니 B.가 만들어 낸 말로 단어 'mean(못된, 심술궂은)' 뒤에 '-ish'를 붙여 '못돼 보이는', '심술궂게 보이는'이라는 의미의 형용사로 사용하였다.

tattoos[3] on theirselves.

Just then, I sat up in my bed.

'Cause a good idea **pop**ped into my head, that's why!

"Hey, a tattoo is easy to **spot**, I **bet**!" I said. "And so maybe I can find that crook on the **playground** tomorrow!"

After that, I went right straight to sleep. 'Cause I would need my strength for crook-looking.

The next day at **recess**, I didn't play horses with Lucille and that Grace.

Instead, I runned all around the playground looking for the mitten crook.

---

3 **tattoo** 문신. 뾰족한 도구로 피부에 먹물이나 물감을 물들여 글씨나 그림 등을 새긴 것.

Only too bad for me. 'Cause most of the children had their jackets on. And so I couldn't even see any crooks with tattoos.

Pretty soon, the bell rang.

That is when my eyes got tears in them. 'Cause I would never see my mittens again. Not ever, ever, never.

I started walking to Room Nine.

My nose was **sniffling** and **drip**pity.

I **wipe**d it on my **attractive** jacket **sleeve**.

Then—all of a sudden—a pink fluffy girl **skip**ped past me.

She had on a pink fluffy dress. With pink fluffy socks and shoes. And a pink fluffy jacket made of pink fluffy **fur**.

And guess what else?

SHE HAD BLACK **FURRY** MITTENS

IN HER PINK FLUFFY POCKETS!

My eyes got big and wide!

"HEY! MY MITTENS! MY MITTENS! MY MITTENS!" I **scream**ed real loud.

Then I put my head down. And I **zoom**ed at her like a **speed**ing bull.

Mrs. saw me running. She **grab**bed me by my attractive winter jacket.

I jumped up and down and pointed.

"THAT PINK FLUFFY GIRL **STOLE**D MY MITTENS! SHE IS THE CROOK! ONLY HER JACKET IS **COVER**ING UP HER TATTOO! AND SO THAT'S WHAT HAD ME **STUMP**ED!"

Mrs. called to the pink fluffy girl.

She skipped over to where we were.

I kept on jumping.

"YOU STOLED THEM! YOU STOLED MY MITTENS!" I said.

"No, I didn't," she said back. "I didn't steal anything. I *found* these mittens. They were right in the grass. And so I thought nobody wanted them."

"I did!" I **yell**ed. "I wanted them! My grampa Miller bought them for no good reason. And I have been worrying about them all day. And all night. And that is called **heartache**, madam![4]"

Mrs. said to **hush** my voice.

She took my mittens away from the pink fluffy girl. And gave them back to me.

Then she **bend**ed down. And she talked to the pink fluffy girl real serious.

"Even if you thought no one wanted these mittens, it was wrong of you to take them," she told her.

The pink fluffy girl pointed at me.

"But she didn't even **take** good **care of** them," she said.

---

4 **madam** '계집애'라는 뜻으로 건방진 여자아이를 얕잡아 부를 때 사용하는 비격식적인 호칭.

I **stamp**ed my foot.

"Yes, I did! I did too take care of them! I left them with my attractive winter jacket. 'Cause I didn't even know there was crooks at this place!"

Mrs. said *hush* to me again.

"You should have taken them to the Lost and Found," she told the pink fluffy girl.

"Yeah! 'Cause then I would have found them when I looked there!" I said. "And so what do you think that box is there for? My health?"

The pink fluffy girl started to cry.

"But I really, really love them," she said.

Mrs. **smooth**ed her hair.

"I'm afraid that's not the **issue**," she

said.

"Yeah, we're afraid that's not the issue," I said. "'Cause *Finders keepers* isn't the rule, apparently. And so from now on, if you find my **stuff**, you have to take it to the Lost and Found. Plus also you can put it in my grampa's **mailbox**."

Mrs. looked at me a real long time.

She said I am getting on her **nerve**s.

After that, she held the pink fluffy girl's hand. And they went to talk to her teacher.

I quick put my mittens on.

Then I **buried** my face in their black furry fur.

And I danced around real **joyful**.

8
I Am Not a Crook

The next day, I went to **Principal**'s office.

The **grouchy typing** lady looked over the **counter** at me.

I **rock**ed **back and forth** on my feet.

"Yeah, only I'm not even bad, again," I said. "I just need to go to the Lost and Found, and **that's all**."

The grouchy typing lady opened up the **closet**. She pulled out the big box.

Just then, the phone rang. And she hurried up to answer it.

I quick **bend**ed down and **dig**ged my hands in the Lost and Found.

Then my heart got very **thrill**ed. 'Cause I saw that wonderful teddy **backpack** again, that's why!

I **snuggle**d my face in his **tummy**.

"Mmm . . . I still love this softy guy," I **whisper**ed.

I put him on my back and **skip**ped all around.

The grouchy typing lady **hang**ed **up** the phone.

"Did you lose that, too?" she asked me. "Is that why you're here?"

I kept on standing there and standing

there.

"Wellll?" she said.

Finally, I did a big **sigh**.

Then I walked very slow back to the box. And I took off the teddy backpack.

"No," I said. "Not why."

After that, I **reach**ed in my pocket. And I pulled out my wonderful pen.

"I found this," I said. "It was on the floor by the **water fountain**. And I really, really love it. Only that is not the **issue**."

Then I did a big, deep breath. And I dropped my wonderful pen into the Lost and Found.

"I am not a crook," I said kind of quiet.

The grouchy typing lady looked nicer at me. She **ruffle**d my hair.

"No," she said. "Of course you're not a crook."

After that, I rocked back and forth on my feet some more. And I waited and waited and waited.

The typing lady raised up her **eyebrows** at me.

"I'm waiting for the **grin**," I explained. "Only there seems to be a **delay**."

She laughed right out loud.

That's when I felt it.

The grin.

It came right on my face!

"Hey! It's working! It's working!" I said real **squealy**.[1]

I skipped all around the office very happy.

Then the typing lady opened up the door. And I skipped **all the way** to Room Nine.

And guess what?

I didn't even find a pen that writes four different colors!

And that was a big **relief**!

---

1 **squealy** 주니 B.가 만들어 낸 말로 단어 'squeal(꽥 소리를 지르다)'의 뒤에 '-y'를 붙여 '꽥꽥거리며'라는 의미의 부사로 사용하였다.